Dare to Let Go

Also by Alexandra Vasiliu

Healing Is a Gift
Healing Words
Time to Heal
Be My Moon
Blooming
Magnetic
Plant Hope
Through the Heart's Eyes

Dare to Let Go

Poems about Healing
and Finding Yourself

Alexandra Vasiliu

Stairway Books
Boston

Dare to Let Go: *Poems about Healing and Finding Yourself* by Alexandra Vasiliu. Boston, Stairway Books, 2022

Editing services provided by Melanie Underwood at
www.melanieunderwood.co.uk
Cover Illustrations: Rusyn via www.shutterstock.com
Book Illustrations: Dychkova Natalya via www.shutterstock.com

ISBN-13: 9798352539453

*For all those who believe
in the power of letting go*

Contents

Alexandra Vasiliu

Dare to Let Go

Your Healing Story

If you read this book,
you are trying to write your story.
A story about self-forgiveness
and self-acceptance.
A story about finding inner peace
and light.
A story about embracing yourself
through change.
A story about welcoming
the unknowns of life
with an open heart.
You will accept
that you are not in control of anything.
You will realize
that you know nothing,
and that is okay too.

You will learn
how to cope with uncertainty
and crave peace.
You will discover
many unbelievable things about yourself.
You will learn
how to become comfortable in yourself
and with yourself again.
But let me tell you a secret –
letting go will be part
of your healing story
and it will be one
of the most important chapters of all.
You will learn
that letting go should be
a one-way street –
only forward.
Now,
my friend,
make the first step
and gather the courage
to let go of everything
that stops you from changing
and evolving.

A Lovely Inner Garden

When you release your burdens,
you start planting
the seeds of your healing.
You start gardening your heart
and turn it into fertile soil.
Be patient.
Don't force the change.
Growth and healing are delicate siblings
that cannot be separated.
They come slowly.
It will take time
to see growth inside your heart
and admire the vibrant flowers
that you planted within.
Stay peaceful every day.
Stay attuned to your healing,

and enjoy the privilege
of being part
of your significant transformation.
Eventually,
you will celebrate
the blooming season
in each corner of your heart.
You will have a lovely garden.
A lovely inner garden.

Reclaim Your Power

Has anyone ever told you
that letting go is not about failure?
Letting go is not a journey of loss,
blame,
or grief.
Letting go is a journey
that starts with self-awareness
and ends with self-respect.
It is a journey of healing,
finding yourself,
and reclaiming your strength.
Dare to believe in yourself.
You are such a beautiful soul.
You only need more courage and clarity
to learn
how to move on confidently,

without training wheels
or constant support.
Don't be afraid.
Letting go is not a destination
or a long road going nowhere.
Letting go is the beginning
of your evolution.
Embrace this change.
You will reclaim your life,
your power,
your heart.
You will end up incorporating
the most empowering word
in the world –
dare.
So, my friend,
this is why I tell you:
dare to let go,
dare to fight,
dare to heal,
dare to dream,
dare to make a change,
dare to hope,
dare to grow,

dare to find yourself,
dare to reclaim your heart,
dare to build a happy life.
Just *dare*, my friend.
Victory is for the brave souls,
and you are one of them,
a fabulous and fearless eagle.

Bravery

Sometimes,
bravery means
choosing to forgive.
Forgive yourself
for not doing enough,
for not making more good things possible,
for being apathetic too often.
Forgive yourself
for not contributing enough
to spread love, peace, and light
into your relationship,
your family,
your community,
your small *world*.
Forgive yourself
and strive to become the person

you have always wanted to be.
Then,
forgive the people around you
for all the good things
they could have done
and didn't.
Sometimes,
bravery means
saying out loud,
'I forgive you.'
Then, let these words flow,
along with your tears,
into the river of love.

Repeat After Me

Constant healing starts
when you embrace
the power of letting go.
If you need this reminder,
I hope
you will heal
in time.
I hope
someday,
you will love your life again.
Until then,
please accept my words
and repeat after me,
'Constant healing starts
when you embrace
the power of letting go.'

Don't Be Afraid

Don't be afraid of your light.
Let go of your insecurities.
Your heart is a magnificent star.
Let your brightness shine gracefully.
Let your magical voice sing of love
and add meaning
to the world's splendor.
Don't be afraid of your light.
Your heart is unique –
a beautiful universe,
a glowing cosmos,
a magnificent star.

A Dead Place

Dare to let go of your traumatic past.
It is a dead place
devasted by your inner wars.
You will never live there again.
Who can ever make a home
somewhere
where there is nothing beautiful left?

On Your Own

The most difficult moment
in a damaged relationship
is not about saying goodbye
or letting go of the person you once loved.
It is the particular moment
when you realize
that you will no longer be
a stranger to grief.
For a while,
you will be on your own.
For a while,
you will share your heart's room
with hurt.
Stay brave.

Alexandra Vasiliu

For Those Who Feel Hopeless

If you feel down and hopeless,
remind yourself
that letting go of your past
is not an overnight process.
It takes time.
Pray
to have more patience and resilience.
Spend more time
reflecting on
what you have been through in your life
and what you want to do from now on.
Spend more time
decluttering your soul
from toxic things.
Spend more time
forgiving,

understanding your wounded self,
accepting your raging feelings,
and revamping self-respect.
Spend more time
investigating your aspirations
and emotional needs.
Spend more time praying.
God will help you.
He will send you the clarity
that you need.
Pray to have more inner strength
to let go of the bad habits
that brought you here.
Become more purposeful
by letting go of your past.
Work hard to move on
and see the change
unfolding in your heart.
Discover all the good things
that could make your heart flourish.
Grow consciously
with courage and determination.
Never give up.
You will witness miracles

that will touch your life forever.
You will build
a beautiful, bright inner identity.
But right now,
keep moving on –
this is the bravest thing
you can do for yourself.

The Art of Letting Go

Letting go will teach you the art
of being gentle and humble,
yet powerful and free.
The less you control,
the more you grow with wisdom.
Learn the art of letting go.
Work on yourself assiduously,
and you will come to appreciate
all the things
that matter in the fullness of time.

When You Decide

When you decide
to let go of your past
and change your life,
you will experience
a moment of epiphany.
You will realize that
love and peace are not abstract concepts
but the arms of God
that can heal your vulnerable self.
His hands can bandage
your invisible wounds
and help you rise from ashes.
You will realize that
in life,
all the essential changes fulfill you
spiritually.

From that day on,
you will be ready
to go forward,
to heal,
and become a kinder soul.

Free Yourself

If you are trapped inside yourself,
in the midst of disturbing experiences,
remember my words:
you can't spend your life
tortured by pain.
Fight to free yourself.
Demolish the prison of grief.
Turn complex circumstances
into something simple
and meaningful.
Fight.
There are so many people
around you
who want to see you happy again.
Fight.
Get out of your inner jail.

Fight for the day
when you look outside
and admire a sunny morning.
You will see a reflection
of your beautiful, golden soul.

The Wisdom of Simplicity

If you want to let go of your past
and move on effortlessly,
you must adopt good habits.
Start with something
that gives you inner peace.
Take a walk in the woods.
Admire a lovely sunrise
and catch a fiery sunset.
Let a soft breeze calm you down
and touch your heart.
Go to the ocean
and listen to the waves' music.
Cherish the moments
with your friends.
Spend more time around kids –
they are so good at showing us

that life is made only of the present time.
Slowly but surely,
you will figure out
what are the good habits
that you want to adopt into your life.
Slowly but surely,
you will grasp the gentleness
that is behind insignificant things.
You will find the poetry of simplicity
and rejoice in finding yourself in it.
You will nourish your mind
with candor and clarity.
Slowly but surely,
you will have the ability
to let go of your past
and move on effortlessly.
Slowly but surely,
you will embrace harmony
and say to yourself,
'I will stay rooted
in the wisdom of simplicity,
for this is the true art of letting go.'

The Power of Letting Go

When you let go of something
that is toxic to you,
your heart is affirming:
'I want to demolish
all the obstacles that stop me
from growing with grace,
mindfulness,
and understanding.
I want to put an end to anything
that keeps me in darkness,
selfishness,
and ignorance.
I want to let go of anything
that wastes my potential.
From this day on,
I will search for light,

peace,
and healing.
I will educate myself
to recognize
what is emotionally healthy for me.
I will unapologetically build
a new home
for my feelings.
I will choose
love and mental strength
to be the vigorous pillars
of my new home.
I will hold onto hope,
and make it the roof
of my intimate place.
From this day on,
I will gather the courage
to embrace the power of letting go,
so the home of my heart will be
a place
of strength,
serenity,
and hope.'

Never Said

I wished so much
you could tell me,
'Don't be afraid
to show me your heart's wounds.
I want to see how fragile you are.
I want to know what you need the most,
so I can love you
with all my might.
I want to heal you with my love.'
But you never said these words.
You just left me.
I buried those uplifting phrases
in my heart,
and thought
that someday, somehow,
they could grow

and bear the sweet fruits of love.
To my surprise,
all I did was
to desperately wait for you.
My imagination ran on autopilot.
I didn't pay attention
to what happened beneath my skin.
I forgot about my emotional needs.
I lived disconnected from my heart
until I decided
to make a hard choice
and change my life.
I dug out those words
that meant the world to me,
and let them fly away.
They were the words
that you never said to me.
They were the words
that only my imagination had fueled.
You had no intention of telling me
kind, beautiful words.
You just passed through my life
and never intended
to come back.

I decided to let go of your memory
and all your unspoken words,
to save my life.
I knew
if I had kept those words in my heart,
they would have hurt me.
On that day,
I stopped living in my head.
'Fly away, healing words.
Soar into the sky,
make a nest beyond clouds,
somewhere where the dreams come from.
You were not meant to be offered to me.
Fly away.'
It was the secret key
to freeing myself.
I stepped forward
and tried to overcome fantasies,
false assumptions,
unrealistic projections,
imaginary declarations,
and prolonged chaos.
I outgrew you.
And that was the sign

to completely let you go.
I moved on.
'One day,
someone will tell me healing words.
One day,
someone will love me
and heal my heart
with kind, beautiful words.
One day,
someone will fly with me.
One day,
someone will take me beyond clouds,
somewhere where the dreams come from.
One day,
someone will choose to stay with me.'

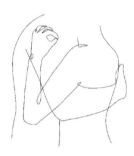

Open the Door to Your Heart

Don't be scared or intimidated
when someone slams the door
in your face.
Rejection will give you
a new perspective on things.
Much of life is made of letting go.
Rejection will teach you
how deeply you need to heal.
Let go of anger –
it is a waste of life and energy.
Learn to be like a summer rain –
cascade quickly over things,
pour out kindness
with everything you do,
with everyone you encounter.
Forgive warmly,

don't leave traces of your gracious self
on any evil thing.
Wash out all the hurt,
and forget easily.
Step by step,
you will plant the seeds of belonging.
Step by step,
you will learn to belong
to your beautiful soul.
This is when
you will realize
that when someone slams the door
in your face,
the door to your heart will open.

Hold your dignity,
embrace your delicate heart,
and practice letting go of any soiled thing.
Remember,
you are the only one
who has the key to your heart.
You are the only one
who knows the onward road.
You are the only one
who has the key to your healing.
You are the only one
who has the key to profound wisdom.

Take You Away

Let go of worries and problems
for a moment.
Close your eyes
and let your dreams take you away
to a peaceful place.

A place made of love
and positive emotions.
A place where you are accepted
as you are.
A place where you can be hugged,
healed,
forgiven,
and renewed with joy.
A place where you can start your life
once again.
Now,
open your heart's eyes
and ask yourself,
'Can I find this place?'

Not Safe

If your loved one neglects you,
you are not safe.
You enter a dangerous area.
Their behavior is a warning sign
that you are not enough.
You should be aware
that ugly things might happen at any time.
Let go of that abusive person.

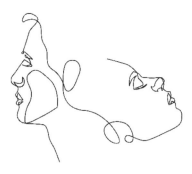

You deserve love and devotion.
Simple and pure.
True and wild.
Sincere and committed.
Nothing less.
You deserve a loyal, loving soul
who believes
that you are not only enough.
You deserve to be everything
to someone extraordinary.

In Love

When you investigate a relationship,
ask yourself,
'Has God been part of this friendship?
Has God been invited to this love?'
If so,
you will learn something more profound
about love,
life,
time,
and faith.
You will find more connection
and wisdom
in nurturing this complex relationship.
You will stay honest and humble.
If not,
it will be easier for you

to let go of that unhealthy relationship.
Remember,
love is not a relationship
between just two souls.
In love,
there is God too.

The Same Speed

While you prepare to let go of your past,
I pray
you can hear the voice of hope
whispering in your ear,
'You are strong.
You are already strong.'
Don't cover that voice.
You can't be stuck in grief.
You can't live in fear.
Life goes on.
Open your heart –
slowly, slowly,
at the same speed
that you release your past.
Accept
that you are fighting with something

that is already dead –
your past.
Accept that.
You cannot live with something dead
inside you,
for eventually,
it will rot your heart.
Let go of it.

'You are brave.
You are strong.'
Forgive yourself

for all the mistakes
that you made.
Stop blaming yourself
for everything that has happened
and for everything that has not happened.
Let go of your past.
Slowly,
slowly.
Look at the corpse of your past –
the waters of acceptance will swallow it.
'You are brave.
You are strong.'
Exit your comfort zone,
leave the familiar area
of your current situation,
and prepare yourself
to face uncertainty.
Don't underestimate your courage –
choosing yourself is the bravest journey
of all.

A Toxic Relationship

After your breakup,
there will still be moments
when you miss your loved one.
Accept your emotions
as they come and go.
Don't fool yourself.
Your emotions are just emotions.
They don't validate anything else
except that you loved them.
In the end,
a toxic relationship remains what it was.

Three Prisoners

When change knocks at your door,
you will release three prisoners
who lived inside your soul:
your bitter voice
that blamed others for your failures,
your angry ego
that played the victim card,
and your inflated self
who thought
that no one loved you enough.
Don't let these terrible inmates dictate
the chapters of your new life.
Say goodbye to your past.
Meet your true self.
Spend time discovering
and appreciating your worth.

Heal your wounds,
and allow joy to have a strong voice
in the story of your future.

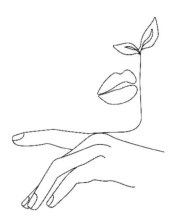

It Is Liberating

Letting go is a gift
that you give yourself.
You free yourself
from all toxic dependences.
It is liberating.
You let go of the person
who didn't love you back.
You let go of your past.
You let go of your insecurities.
And you give yourself the gift
of freedom,
self-love,
healing,
and hope.
You make room for yourself,
for your forgotten dreams,

for your aspirations.
You give yourself a gift.
The gift of a new life,
a new beginning,
a new chance of happiness.

Taking Risks

If you are afraid of letting go,
you are scared of life.
You fear moving on.
You fear being hurt again.
You fear taking risks.
But has anyone ever told you
that fear comes from
the register of unhealthy emotions?
Fear paralyzes all good intentions.
Fear wants you to be a prisoner
of your turbulent mind.
Let go of your anxieties.
Don't get stuck in fear and indecision.
Be brave and overcome your anxieties.
Don't give up on yourself.
Keep healing and fighting for yourself.

Every struggle will help you forge
the person
that you want to become.
Remember,
there is no need for you to be perfect –
just be imperfectly brave every day.

Much More

If someone left,
neglected,
or rejected you,
remind yourself
that you are much more than
a dysfunctional relationship.
Fight to not lose your kindness,
your empathy,
and compassion
through this life experience.
Don't let your past get in your way.
Be a light in the darkness.
Don't allow yourself to be stigmatized
by your emotional trauma.
This turmoil can't control your heart,
yet the fire of suffering can refine you.

Be strong.
Don't beg for affection.
You can't meet true love
in this way.
Say farewell to that abusive person
and discover your healing pathway.
Invite God to restore
your broken heart,
your self-esteem,
your trust in people.
Invite God to show you
the direction
you should follow.
Your healing journey will be proof
that light always conquers darkness.

Be Honest with Yourself

Letting go is not about accepting
that you don't have control
over anyone and anything.
Letting go is not about renouncing
something or someone.
Letting go is about having
the courage to walk away
from a damaged relationship.
Letting go is about releasing
yourself or your partner
from a false connection.
Letting go is about facing the truth.
Letting go is about sincerity.
Letting go is about breaking
the chain of lies.
Letting go is about seeing the reality

as it is.
Letting go is a heroic act –
you choose to be honest
with your heart.
You stop lying to yourself.
Letting go is about the determination
that you want to invest
to end a precarious situation.
Letting go is about taking a step forward.
Letting go is about embracing
the transition
to a new chapter of your life.
Don't be afraid.
There is strength
in facing the truth.
There is strength
in choosing to be honest with yourself.
There is strength
in choosing
to have a healthy relationship
with yourself.
There is strength
in choosing yourself
over a deceitful friend.

There is strength
in choosing to reject chaos
and self-destruction.
There is strength
in building robust boundaries
for your emotional health.
There is strength
in choosing to heal
and grow.
There is strength
in choosing to hope
and dream again.
Someday,
you will understand
there is also much wisdom
in letting go.
Now it is time for the first step –
let go.
Silence your mind,
take a deep breath,
and choose to be honest with yourself.

Sweet Little Flowers

Letting go is not easy.
There will be moments
when memories of your past
will pop up in your mind
and trigger
an avalanche of painful emotions.
Don't run.
Don't leave yourself alone –
pain can weigh heavily on your heart.
Yield your thoughts to God
and pray for His help.
He can teach you how to let go tenderly.
He can guide your path
toward light and peace.
Make God your friend
in this healing journey.

Be strong,
patient,
and perseverant.
Let pain be the wild, rough soil
for your transformation.
Sweet little flowers can grow
in the arid ground,
and so can you.

Rising from Ashes

When you let go of someone
who didn't love you back,
you feel worthless.
You want to cry in the rain,
so no one can see your tears.
You want to run somewhere
far away
where no one knows you.
You want to stop someone
in the street
and ask,
'Excuse me,
is this the way to nowhere?'
My friend,
pain is a country
that I also visited a long time ago.

Allow yourself to grieve,
but don't spin negative thoughts
round and round
in your mind.
Don't descend into a downward spiral.
Discern when something is excessive
and start to control yourself.
When someone didn't love you back,
remind yourself that
God always loves you.
When someone didn't love you back,
remind yourself that
you can seed kindness
in your open wounds,
so you can heal.
You are never worthless.
God endowed you with beautiful gifts
and unique talents.
Have you discovered them all?
Dare to recognize and appreciate
your uniqueness.
Dare to fight
for your dreams and aspirations.
Dare to trust God more.

And next time,
when you want to stop someone
in the street,
dare to ask,
'Excuse me,
where is the direct route to a new life?'
Maybe that person will smile at you
or think that you are crazy.
It is not relevant.
It is important
that God gave you the courage
to feel responsible for yourself.
You will make a change
in your life,
for you will realize
how much you matter.
You will build a new life
for your heart,
for your dreams
and ambitions.
You will never allow yourself
to feel worthless.

The Language of Honesty

Letting go is the language of honesty
that you speak to yourself,
after all the curtains fall
and you remain alone
on the stage
of your life.

Finding Yourself

Letting go is the art
of finding yourself
after you released the one
who meant everything to you,
yet was not meant to be yours.

Not Meant for You

When you let go of someone
who couldn't treat you right,
you follow your heart
that kept whispering to you,
'This is not your soulmate.
This is not your soulmate.'
Now,
trust your gut instincts
and discard the idea
of how things should have been
between you two.
While you face the naked truth –
your *forever* was just a fleeting moment,
please remind yourself
that you are always worthy of love.

Take This Responsibility

Letting go is about taking responsibility
for yourself,
for your heart,
for your emotional health,
for your desires,
for your future.
Letting go is about realizing
that you matter.
Today and always.

A Process of Growth

Letting go is part
of your transformation process.
You will change yourself
when you understand
that life is made of
many endings and deaths.
You will grow
when you learn
how to navigate those endings
and emotional deaths.
You will become kinder
when you learn
how to turn suffering into hope.
You will help others
and often put their needs before yours
when you understand

how great it is to cross a bridge
and not to run through a muddy valley.
Everything that you do
will be proof
that you let go of your old self,
you changed,
you mended your heart,
you outgrew your brokenness,
and became a healing soul
in this ruthless world.
You changed yourself beautifully.
Inside and out.

Going Through a Tunnel

Letting go is a tunnel.
You leave your past behind
and head toward the light.
You enter this tunnel as a child
and exit as a mature soul.
Don't be afraid.
You don't go through this tunnel
for applause,
fame,
or social validation.
You only need to change your life
and move forward.
My friend,
your life is a long chain of changes.
You can't return to your past,
but you can revisit it

from time to time,
so you will heal undeviatingly.
Don't stay trapped in grief.
Embrace change.
Be brave
and enter this tunnel of uncertainty
with faith
in a new beginning.
Something beautiful will welcome you.
Now,
don't stop.
You already know
that this is the way —
the only way toward the future.
Your future.
Your story.
Your life of happiness.

Choosing to Heal Yourself

Letting go is not about
turning your heart into a cemetery
for all the people
that you once loved.
Letting go is about choosing
to heal yourself
while you forgive all the people
that you once loved.

Having Trouble with Letting Go?

If you have trouble with letting go,
please reflect on my words.
Letting go is not an abandonment.
Letting go is an act of courage –
you place yourself into the orbit
of a new beginning.
Hope will be your only universe.
You will not be able
to return to your old self
or leap into the future.
You will only have one thing to do –
to find your heart
in this great, unknown, dark present.

You Learn

Letting go is a way of becoming whole –
you reclaim yourself.
You learn how to be
emotionally healthy and mature.
You learn how to be
strong,
safe,
humble,
and free again.
You learn how to be complete
without chasing illusions.
You learn how to stand up for yourself.
Letting go is a way of embracing yourself
wholeheartedly.

Don't Act Like a Victim

When you let go,
strive not to act
like a victim.
Remember that
when you break free
from a toxic, dysfunctional relationship.
You are not a victim –
you are the owner of your life.
You have choices,
and the first choice is you.
Strip away the layers of
your dead relationship
the same way
you would peel a mandarin,
and keep the sweetest part
for yourself.

Sometimes,
self-love is a hidden treat.
Savor it.
Enjoy it.
You deserve it.

No Perfect Life

Let go of the idea of what a perfect life is.
There is no perfect life.
Go beyond this artificial notion.
There are just imperfect, beautiful lives.
Know yourself.
Build a genuine identity.
Your soul needs purity
to thrive
and shine.

Build Self-Awareness

If someone lets you down,
don't hide away your pain.
Forgive that person
and more importantly,
forgive yourself
for not training your heart to see.
Don't quit on yourself
grieving for someone
who couldn't love you.

Set boundaries
and detach yourself from that wound.
Then run to your inner child
who needs love,
devotion,
and loyalty.
Hug your soul
and whisper softly
'You are loved.'
Forget everything else
in that secret, warm embrace.

A Non-Judgmental Art

Letting go should be an art.
A non-judgmental art,
where you learn
how to avoid negative thoughts,
how to stop blaming yourself
and criticizing a certain someone.
Letting go should be an art
where you learn
how to crawl
from the hell of the past,
and how to have a zigzag run
amid difficult circumstances.
Letting go should be an art
taught in schools
where you learn
how to maintain robust mental health

throughout your life,
how to overcome hurdles,
how to never give up,
how to look inside your heart
with love, compassion, and respect,
and how to appreciate all the progress
that you have already made.
Letting go should be an art
included in all subjects
where you learn
that you are not entitled
to have everything that you want –
some things are not meant to be yours,
and that is fine too.
Be humble, my friend.
You are not forever on earth,
and you can't have everything
that you wish for.
You don't live
in a children's fairy tale.

A Crossroads in Life

The moments of letting go are crossroads
in your life.
You can choose to be stuck
in grief,
despair,
and denial.
Or you can choose to move forward,
search for hope,
and heal yourself.
Follow the path
that offers you the fewest regrets.
The path
that unveils
how strong you are.

Look at the Trees' Leaves

If you want to learn the art of letting go,
look at the trees' leaves –
they drop in the fall,
and the wind carries them away.
No anger,
no resentments arise.
It is what it is –
a time for death,
a time for a new cycle,
a time for a new beginning.
Now,
try to imitate those leaves
when suffering pierces your heart.
Detach yourself from all that withers you
like the leaves separate themselves
from branches.

Let go gently of anything
that stops you from growing.
Be patient and humble.
Life has tens of seasons.
Now,
you enter the season of letting go,
you welcome the season
of finding your own path.
One day,
the season of love will hold your name
and the air will be filled with magic.
You will step straight into tenderness.
One day,
your heart will blossom again.

Only True Love

If someone says to you,
'You came into my life
at the wrong time.
I can't love you.
I am not ready for commitment,'
don't react angrily.
Take a deep breath.
Stop yourself from crying
and remember
that you can't control
how others feel about you.
Stay calm.
Don't harbor resentments.
Think seriously about
what you wish for from now on.
Do you want

to continue this abusive relationship?
You already know
that your partner can't give you
everything you deserve.
You should admit
that you are in a relationship
that drains you emotionally.
You are in the midst of mayhem
and heading for disaster.
It is time to walk away
from this unhealthy relationship.
It is time.
You have to let go.

Build healthy boundaries
to preserve your emotional safety
and your mental health.
Be gentle with yourself
and firm with your partner.
You don't need excuses.
You just need love and affection.
You need a mature relationship,
so you can feel valued and appreciated.
You need a beautiful life
and someone with whom you
can build a bright future.
You don't need excuses.
Remind yourself
that in love,
in true love,
no one can say,
'You came into my life
at the wrong time.
I can't love you.
I am not ready for commitment.'
In love,
in true love,
there is no scarcity of kindness

and devotion.
In love,
in true love,
nobody kills the soul of the other person.
So, hold your tears.
Don't confront your partner.
Keep your head up.
Your soul still wears a crown.
Please don't let it fall.

Walk away.
Remind yourself
that you are still beautiful and precious.
You deserve someone
who can create poetry and music
in your heart.
Take a deep breath.
Allow yourself to rest for a moment.
And then,
exit this nightmare.

Grow Flowers from Your Past

If you believe,
just like me,
that words are healing tools
that mend wounded hearts,
surround yourself
with beautiful expressions
and powerful affirmations.
Heal your heart
with loving,
welcoming,
invigorating words.
Say to yourself,
'Dear Heart,
You are my cozy, warm home.
I love you.
And I love looking at life

through your bright windows.
This is why
I am so willing
to empower you
with kindness.
I will erase all the cruel words
that you have ever heard.
I will eliminate them
with the gentle power
of forgiveness.
I will plant healing words
in your scars
and wait for a miracle to happen.
I know
that you are so strong and marvelous,
that one day,
you will grow flowers from your past.
Dear Heart,
I love you.'

The To-Do List for Letting Go

Detach yourself from toxic relationships.
Connect yourself
to your emotional needs.
Take a long journey of self-discovery.
Show love and compassion to yourself.
Nurture your dreams.
Pray.
Make room for hope.
Forgive.
Forget.
Heal.
Recharge your soul.
Take long walks in nature.
Be there for your friends.
Surround yourself with kind people.
Be patient.

Alexandra Vasiliu

Seed flowers
in a garden
or in your soul.

Give flowers to someone
that you appreciate.
Buy roses for yourself.
Seed dreams
wherever you go.
Radiate healing energy.
Inspire someone
to fulfill their dreams.
Fight hard.
Forgive more.
Move forward.

Let go of stupid distractions.
Stop wasting your time.
Make something meaningful
of your life.
Fill your heart with beauty.
Include 'no' in your vocabulary –
both 'no' and 'yes' come from God.
Maintain healthy boundaries.
Honor your aspirations
and strive to accomplish them.
Help people take their dreams further.
Pray.
Make your heart a safe place.
Keep a positive mindset.
Set a noble life purpose.
Live a deliberate, peaceful life.
Come back to the core of
what always matters –
your soul.
Guard your inner pearl gracefully.
And dare to love again.

A Heartbeat

Self-love is not a lifeless word.
You can hear its heartbeats
in the body of your wounds.
Let go of the hurt, my friend.
Self-love will ignite your hopes
for a better future.

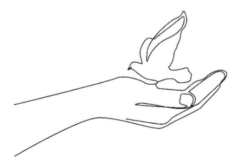

Rule Number One

In love,
don't expect to be chosen.
In love,
you have the right to choose as well.
Let go of negative thoughts
and treat yourself with respect.

Being More Selective

Letting go will teach you
the wisdom of being more selective
with people.
You will put your heart into the hands
of those who know
how to protect an orchid
without breaking it.

Not Blind

Love is not blind.
Open wide the eyes of your heart
and look at the person
in front of you.
Do you think
that this person is your soulmate?
Do you feel understood,
protected,
and well-loved by your friend?
Do you find your peace
when you two are together?
Do you two crave to share
the same space
at the same time?
Love is *not* blind.
Open wide the eyes of your heart

and choose wisely.
Look straight at the soul
of the person
you love.
Accept any truth
that you see.
If this person is not the right one,
your heart will tell you.
Let go of that relationship
without drama.
Be wise.
Remember,
love is not a Hollywood movie
or a thirty-minute performance.
You are not on a theater stage
and no one is watching you,
so open wide the eyes of your heart
and choose wisely.
Love is not blind.

Time to Grow

Let go of unfulfilling relationships.
Hold your dignity,
and remind yourself
that it is time for you
to embrace growth.
Drop the anchor of your heart
into the waters of self-reflection.
Allow yourself to stay there for a while.
Don't rush.
Mooring is part of self-discovery.
You need time to process things
and figure out
what kind of love
you want.
Soak up all the wisdom and spirituality
that you yearn for –

your heart asks for substance.
One day,
you will gain a mature vision of love,
happiness,
connection,
and togetherness.
One day,
you will know
what your heart truly needs.
One day,
you will start sailing
new oceans,
into the sea of life.
And you will sail and sail
for months and months
until you see
a new horizon.
On that day,
you will anchor at a beautiful dock,
where love is not only a feeling.
You will give a name
to that beautiful port,
a secret name
that will say everything

about your search.
And from that day on,
your heart will savor an abundance
of blessings and peace.

No Anesthesia

Letting go is like surgery
without anesthesia.
You extract your heart
from the body
of a toxic relationship,
and try to put it back
inside your chest.
You didn't expect
that you would cry and mourn so much.
Nobody told you
that suffering would not lessen easily.
Nobody told you
that after letting go,
you were supposed to grieve,
walk,
and live without any anesthesia.

A Deep Breath

It is hard to let go of your painful past
when your trauma is written everywhere
on the ramparts of your soul.
How can you come out of this chaos,
rise from the ashes,
and move forward?
You feel dead inside,
before your death.
Don't give up.
Don't deny yourself emotionally.
Letting go is a four-letter word,
spelled *hope*.
First,
wipe away your emotional hurt,
erase every inch of darkness,
and paint the inside of your enclosure

with the colors of love,
compassion,
and self-acceptance.
Then,
every morning,
be assertive
and remind yourself,
'I will heal.
And I want to feel positive about that.'
Allow yourself to emerge
from tenebrosity.
Let your beautiful light shine
increasingly
every day of your life.
Remember,
letting go is a four-letter word,
spelled *hope*.
Spread light.
Never give up.
Reclaim your inner beauty,
your innocence,
your hidden poetry.

A Cathartic Act of Breathing

Letting go is a cathartic act of breathing.
You exhale grief and inhale hope.
Hope that you will heal.
Hope that you will move on.
Hope that you will find someone
who can cherish you completely.

Wait

You tried everything
to make someone
love you,
yet nothing worked.
Has anybody told you
that in true love,
you don't have to do anything
to be well-loved?
Stop bending over backward
for someone
who treats you miserably.
Stop being loyal to someone
who is absent
from your life.
Stop being kind to someone
who minimizes your worth.

You are not free
when someone is abusive.
Let that person go.
Break the chains of lies
and free yourself
from this pseudo-relationship.
Wait for someone
who will place the royal crown of love
on your heart.
Wait for someone
who doesn't need proof
of how beautiful you truly are.
Wait in a constructive,
positive way –
heal your wounds,
take care of your inner self,
and do whatever you need to do
to mend your heart
and be ready for true love.
Remember,
letting go is an invitation
to improve the relationship
with your innocent self,
and determine your priorities in life.

The Right Balance

Sometimes,
it is hard
to find the right balance
between not hurting someone
and not hurting yourself.
This is when you should pray more
to embrace the power of letting go.
Look beyond appearances.
Let go of those
who consume your energy
and never give back anything precious.
Let go of them.
Close the door of your heart.
Don't slam it.
Close it gently.
This way

you will not hurt anyone,
or yourself.
You don't have to live
as though you have something
to prove to people
or to the world.
No, you don't.
Be responsible for your soul.
Return to yourself.
Be meek and humble.
Fill your heart
with peace
and wisdom.
Embark on a journey
toward self-awareness.
You will learn
to manage the balance
between not hurting anyone
and not hurting yourself,
between being too kind to others
and staying strong for yourself.

A Quick Reminder

Letting go is a chance
that you give yourself
to search for the light
that has always been in your heart.
Remember,
until the letting go moment,
you used to look for this light
in other people.
You even waited to see the light
at the end of the tunnel.
But now,
it is time to search for
this wonderful, marvelous light
inside your beautiful self.
You might gleam
sooner than you expect.

Better Things

Don't let go of anything with a hard heart.
Don't blame yourself.
Don't obsess with your past.

Have a reason for hope.
Better things will come.

Don't Give Up

Whenever you try to let go of someone
who hurts you,
remind yourself,
'You are much more than
a damaged relationship.
You are much more than the emptiness
that you feel right now.'
Letting go is the art of recreating yourself.

Give yourself enough time
to become a beautiful, free spirit.
You will learn
how to detach yourself
from harmful people,
rekindle the relationship
with your inner child,
and help your soul grow beautifully.
Don't give up.
There is hope in letting go.
There is beauty in new beginnings.

Two Things

Letting go will teach you
two essential things.
First,
letting go will force you
to return to your inner child.
You will root yourself in self-compassion.
You will discover
that your soul is the best friend
that you have for the rest of your life.
Make this friend your mentor.
Never quit on yourself.
Secondly,
letting go will teach you
how to cultivate
lasting and meaningful connections.
You will know

to set up realistic expectations
for a healthy relationship.
You will learn
how to wait for true love.

Finding Yourself Again

Letting go is a harsh lesson.
You have given
all your good feelings
and all of you
to the wrong person.
Now,
you must return to yourself.
Turn this life lesson into an art.
Take all the time
that you need
to learn
the art of finding yourself.
Allow yourself
to understand the meaning of suffering
at your own pace.
Allow yourself

to feel whatever you want.
If you need to grieve,
just grieve.
If you need to cry,
just cry.
If you need to be quiet,
just be quiet.
If you need to scream,
just scream.
Allow yourself
to accept what went wrong
and what was never meant to be
in your relationship.
Allow yourself
to release what is already dead
inside your heart.
You need to come back to life.
Breathe in this uncertainty.
Embrace yourself
in the chaos of fears.
Give yourself time,
space,
and love.
Don't leave any corner of your heart

untouched,
unloved,
unseen,
unhealed.
You need love
to validate your worth.
Remind yourself,
'I am coming back home.
I am returning to my true self.
I am trying to find
my unique beauty,
my worth,
my purpose in life.
I am coming back home
carrying my wonderful soul
in my arms.
I am coming back to my true self.'
Detach from your past.
Give yourself time,
space,
and love.
Seed hope
on every path
of your inner journey.

Keep learning
how to let go of traumatic experiences.
Stop blaming yourself
for things from before.
Don't overthink your past.
It can make you feel more vulnerable.
Don't make plans for the future.
You can't have everything
figured out at once.
Just be patient now,
for patience is a part
of your growth process.
Be understanding with yourself,
for empathy is a part
of your growth process.
Don't rush your healing.
You have already made essential
progress.
You overcame so many bad experiences.
You cleared your conscience.
Breathe.
Pray.
Say,
'Thank you, Lord, for this moment.

'You helped me come out of the torment.
Thank you, Lord, for my heart
that hasn't turned into granite
or a piece of ice.
I didn't become one
with my excruciating pain,
with my failure,
with my darkness.
I realized
I am alive,
and so, I get a second chance.
I discovered
so many beautiful emotions
inside me.
I discovered
my potential,
my charm,
my dreams.
I want to live intentionally
from now on.
Is there anything greater than
living purposefully
with a pure heart,
full of aspirations?

'Help me, Lord, change my life.
I want to spread love and beauty,
and do it
constantly and continuously,
so I will never be consumed
by depression.
I want to mean something more.
I want to mean love for someone.
I want to matter.
I want to be busy doing
something meaningful
with myself,
and do it
every single day.
I want to bloom again,
and do it
every single moment.
Help me, Lord, rebuild my life.
Please, be with me.
Put a brush in my hands
and guide me to paint
my soul and my life.
I want to love,
and my love be validated
by mutual love.'

What Brave Souls Need the Most

Letting go is not a passive act.
It takes courage to let go
and face your challenges.
It takes courage
to wrap your heart in hope
and move on
beyond unpredictability.
Be understanding with yourself
when you need to hear
an encouraging, healing word.
Don't stop.
Keep being progressive –
that is what brave souls need the most.

Just Dare

If you are heartbroken
and in the process
of healing your wounds,
you might notice
that some days,
grief will unfold its powers
and hit you mercilessly.
Don't step back.
There is only one thing
you should be scared of –
to live without your pure self.
Dare to overcome grief.
Dare to let go of your past.
Dare to heal your wounds.
Dare to move on.
Endings are not always about goodbyes

but about saying 'Hello' and 'Welcome.'
Dare to say 'Hi'
to your restored self.
Hope will fuel your growth.

Not Cutting Out

Letting go is not about cutting people out
of your life.
Letting go is about gathering the strength
to become free
and emotionally mature
while you forgive all the people
that harmed you
in the past.

A Long Process

Has anyone ever told you
that brokenness doesn't disappear
one day
out of the blue?
It usually stays
as long as you allow it
in your life.
This is why you should work on yourself
to regain your life,
your heart,
a purpose in your existence.
Letting go of your past is vital
to your healing journey.
Work on your broken heart, my friend.
Day after day,
week after week,

month after month,
year after year.
Don't let grief push you
to the brink of despair.
Don't let grief consume your heart.
Don't let negative feelings flood
your mind –
they are only visitors
that come and go.
Work on your heart.
Heal your inner emptiness.
Fix your brokenness.
Fill your heart with dreams
and noble aspirations.
Set beautiful goals.
Slowly,
slowly,
you will gain the tenacity
to fight unapologetically
for your soul.
You will become stronger.
You will realize that you matter.
And you have always mattered.

Alexandra Vasiliu

Until There Is Nothing Left

Letting go is not a three-minute story
or a play
where you are the leading actor
slamming the door
behind a failed relationship.
You will not perform a drama
on the stage of your life.
You will not have spectators,
except for your ego.
You will not receive flowers
at the end of the show.
You should realize
that you are experiencing
the most painful awakening
of your life –
the ending of a relationship

that meant so much to you.
You will find yourself betrayed,
vulnerable,
insecure,
scared,
sad,
shy,
lost,
alone,
unwanted,
unloved.
You will often feel depressed.
You will go through
a long and challenging process
of letting go.
You will surprisingly notice
that letting go will continue
long after your last goodbye.
Every day,
you will learn to let go of something
that belonged to your past.
Every day,
you will let go of something
that still consumes your present –

anger,
resentments,
sadness,
despair.
Every day,
you will understand
that it will take time
to release your past
and free yourself
from what was not meant to be.
Every day,
you will learn to accept the new reality
and assimilate the idea
that it is over.
Every day,
you will learn to let go.
Every day,
every day,
every day,
every day,
until there is nothing left
that could bother you
or pain your heart.
And this is what will make you strong.

What You Accepted

When you decide to let go of someone
who didn't love you back,
remind yourself of a few things.
From the very beginning
of this relationship
you chose
to be vulnerable,
honest,
and kind.
You agreed
to respect the other's freedom of choice.
You realized
the importance of not controlling
your loved one.
You accepted the idea
that love is a gift

and not a trade.
Remind yourself of all these things now.
Be honest with yourself.
Be kind to yourself.
Be considerate of your own needs.
Respect your soul.
And exit this abusive relationship
smoothly,
peacefully,
willingly.
If you crush down the pillars of dignity,
you will only hurt yourself.
Your loved one will not love you back.
That person will continue
to neglect you emotionally.
Be wise.
Let go of this dysfunctional relationship.
Don't overthink.
Don't distort the truth.
Don't try to find reasons or excuses.
What reasons can you find
for someone
who didn't love you back

and offered you nothing?
What excuses can you find
for this emotional abuse
and its psychological violence?
Don't lie to yourself.
Don't deny your emotional needs.
Don't distort the current reality.
Don't bend yourself
to the will and the selfish desires
of your partner.
Don't become passive
in your life story.
Accept the present reality,
and let go of this destructive relationship
smoothly,
peacefully,
willingly.
In time,
you will become wiser
and increase the consistency of self-love.
Be patient and kind to yourself.
One day,
you will receive the most precious gift
in the world –
to love and be loved in return.

After Letting Go

After letting go,
take your time to heal.
Don't rush this difficult journey.
Every day
when you wake up,
say,
'Thank you, God,
for giving me this heart.
Small,
yet large enough to feel so many things.
Meek,
yet brave enough to forgive.
Empathetic,
yet strong enough to heal.
Thank you, God,
for creating this daring heart only for me.

'Pain hasn't petrified her,
suffering didn't kill her.
I will keep purifying my sensitive heart –
this is my daily duty.
I hope
one day,
I will help others too.
Thank you, God,
for teaching my heart
what to do
from now on.
Letting go woke up my heart.

'Letting go made me understand
that healing should be part
of my identity,
along with self-love
and self-respect.
Thank you, God,
for opening the eyes of my heart
and seeing my true, precious self.
I am grateful to You
for creating this brave heart
only for me –
I was the one
who needed this gem
the most.'

When You Learn

You will change
when you learn
to let go of old destructive behaviors.
You will grow
when you learn
to stop worshipping the toxic patterns
of your past.
You will thrive
when you learn
to reconcile with your fragile self
and move on with your life.
Don't doubt that, my friend.
You will grow and bloom gracefully,
for you will learn
to make wise choices in life.

An Act of Self-Respect

Letting go is an act of self-respect.
You detach from an unhealthy situation
and treat yourself with dignity.
You honor your soul,
your dreams,
your aspirations,
your hopes.
You set boundaries.
You choose yourself
and pursue the light
that is deeply hidden
in your heart.
Isn't this a sign of inner strength?
Isn't this a sign of self-awareness?
Isn't this proof
of your beautiful evolution?

Teach You

If you want to transform your lover
into someone perfect
from a fairy tale,
stop right now.
Let go of this silly approach.
Love is not about chasing unicorns
or meeting unreasonable expectations.
Let go of all these crazy, unrealistic goals.
Love is about flowing together
over each other's imperfections
and keeping the same target –
to take a sip of happiness
together
every day.
If you want someone perfect
from a fairy tale,

turn yourself into that person.
Transform your inner child,
change your mindset,
work on your volatile feelings,
purify your soul,
heal your injured self,
and transfigure yourself
into a loving soul.
Become a better person
for the sake of your relationship.
Don't just sit and wait for miracles.
Work hard.
Strive to become emotionally mature,
so when you show up in love,
you will be nothing but a blessing.
Peace and harmony will germinate
in your relationship.

What You Don't Know

Everyone says that letting go is freeing,
but no one ever told you
how complicated this process would be.
No one ever told you
how long it would take
to reach inner peace and freedom.
You want to let go of
your relationship
without agony.
You long for normalcy.
You long for a healthy relationship.
You want to cuddle up
with your innocent self again.
How could you attain all these?
No one ever told you
that to be free

you have to live
with the hurt again,
you have to rememorate
all the good, the bad, and the ugly
of your unsuccessful relationship.
You have to pass
through suffering again.
Everyone says
that letting go is freeing,
but no one ever told you
that letting go will prove to you
that there is a thin line
between hell and heaven,
between pain and solace.
And you will have to walk
that line
like a delicate ballerina –
without falling again into
the hell of your trauma.

Give Yourself a Fair Chance

Never allow a futile love story
to hold you back.
Don't let despair destroy your soul.
Allow change to come into your life.
Breathe deeply,
and let go of that relationship.
Accept the response of life –
you deserve much more.
Allow personal transformation to have
a permanent home
in your heart.
You will give yourself a fair chance
to heal and evolve.

Coming Back

Coming back home to your vulnerable
self
is never
a mistake.
Every house needs repairs
and improvements,
and so do you.
Let go of illusions and self-deception.
Start working on your precious self
intentionally,
diligently,
steadily.

New Promises

You can't undo your past.
The only way
you can rewrite your story
is to separate yourself from your toxic
history.
Let it go
and promise to your precious soul,
'I will let go of anything
that stood between our connection.
I will never estrange myself
from you.
I will heal myself,
and I will heal you.
And I will help you grow with wisdom,
for you are my everything.'

You Owe Yourself This Fight

When you feel depressed,
say to yourself,
'I have to get back to life
and fight
steadily
and fiercely
to overcome depression.
I have to let go of the toxic thoughts
that bury me alive.
I have to find the light.
My light.
I owe this fight to God
and to my pure soul.
I will hold on to hope
and find the way back
to the marvels of life.'

Find the light, my friend.
Your light.
Imitate the stars that shine
in the middle of the night.
Don't abandon yourself
in the arms of darkness.
Don't forget your needs
in the chaos of depression.
Examine your heart
under the light of God,
and empower yourself with hope.
Deep down in your heart,
you have beautiful things to offer.
Dare to bring them to life.
Dare to illuminate and inspire.
Dare to live radiantly.
Fight steadily and fiercely
to overcome anything
that stops you from shining.
Fight to overcome depression,
and let hope have the last word.
You owe this incredible fight to God
and to your pure soul.

Carry You Forward

You might have moments
when hope is out of reach.
Those moments are quick reminders
of your human frailty.
Pray to God to empower you with grace.
Be humble and meek.
Let go of your vulnerable thoughts
and emotional insecurity.
Keep a healing word
in the vessel of your soul
for each moment of despair.
Don't fear.
Hope will carry you forward,
and you will heal.
God will unwaveringly help you navigate
to growth.

The Benefits of Letting Go

Letting go is a promise of strength,
courage,
clarity,
and maturity.
A promise
that you make to your resilient self.
You will permit good changes
to come into your life.
You will welcome new habits
in your daily schedule.
You will adjust to change
with a new sense of wonder.
You will ardently work on your mindset.
You will put indomitable perseverance,
zeal,
hope,

sincerity,
and mindfulness
into all your efforts.
You will make a promise that
letting go will not ruin your soul.
Letting go will never leave space
for asking yourself,
'For whom will I live?'
You already know the answer.
Letting go is a promise of strength,
courage,
clarity,
and maturity.
A promise
that you make to your precious child.
'I will live for you, my dear soul,
to heal you
and raise you with love,
with wisdom,
and respect.
I will live for you
and forge a close bond.
I will live for you,
for you have always been

my guiding light.
'I will live for you,
my beautiful soul,
so we can learn together
the way to harmony.'

Stop That Voice

Sometimes
there is a voice
in your mind
that doesn't allow you
to let go of a toxic relationship.
You must say to that sly voice,
'Stop!

'Stop making me feel like a victim.
I want this chaos to end.
I want to live free.
I want to have a beautiful,
peaceful life.'
Repeat these words –
they will cut off all the invisible ties
between you and your loved one.
Don't be afraid.
Letting go is an intentional way
to embrace yourself.
You need your delicate self so much.
Be persistent.
Letting go is a consistent way
to move forward.

Growing

Open your heart
as you would open a magical window.
Look inside
and see
what is not helping you
become spiritually mature.
Then, let go of anything
that steals your strength.

Where There Is a Scar

Where there is a scar,
there is always a wound behind it.
Learn from your emotional faults,
so when you let go of your past,
your healing will bring wisdom.

When You Become a Writer

Letting go is not about ripping
sad chapters
from the book of your past.
Letting go is not about evicting people
from your heart.
Letting go is not about rewriting
the parts of your life
of which you are not proud.

Letting go is about keeping intact
all the pages of your book
while you decide
to become a writer.
From now on,
you will add
meaningful new chapters
to your life book.

Choose One Path

Of all the paths
that you can take in life,
choose the one
that will never make you feel ashamed.
Just that one.
Be brave and honest with yourself.
Embrace the unknown
with faith in God,
and let go of the world's noise.
You will reveal
your authentic, beautiful light.
What could be more fabulous?

Build a Luminous Home

Feelings are part of your anatomy.
The anatomy of your heart.
Don't let sadness be your inner eyes.
Don't let anger be your unseen mouth.
Don't let despair be your inner voice.
Feelings are part of your anatomy.
Let go of negative emotions,
so you can build a unique home
for your heart.
A home of light and love.
A home of dignity and kindness.
A home of healing and peace.
A home of positive, loving feelings.
A home where you can grow wonderfully.

Dare to Let Go

My friend,
dare to let go of anything
that harms you
and holds you back.
Dare to choose your gentle self
when everything around crushes you.
Dare to pray to God
in your most difficult moments.
Dare to humbly ask for help
and thank Him loudly
in your heart.
Dare to heal your wounds
and overcome challenges.
Dare to fight bravely
and rise from misfortunes.
Despite everything

that you have been through,
you are alive.
What could be more impressive than that?
You are alive –
repeat that.
You can turn your life into a poem.
A poem of love and hope.
A poem of change and growth.
A poem of meanings and blessings.
A poem of beauty and serenity.
You are alive,
so you have everything to fight for.
Work on yourself.

Overcome all the hurdles of life.
One day,
when you wake up,
the world will smell of peace
and you will love your life again.
On that day,
you will know
that the world was made for you
as a gift,
and you were created for this world
as a warrior –
to metamorphose failures into strength,
to fight,
to win,
to reclaim your victory,
to shine,
to love,
and eventually
to celebrate
the beautiful, unique *you*.
My friend,
your heart is a poem
and you did everything you could
to prove it.

Dear Reader,

Thank you very much for reading my empowering poetry book, an extension of my soul, to meet you and help you wherever you are.

I hope you found inspiration, solace, peace, hope, love, practical advice, and encouragement.

If so, please take a moment and show your appreciation by writing a brief review on the website where you purchased this book. I think other readers might find your thoughts helpful. Also, your support will help me to write more books like this one.

Thank you very much.

Wishing you the courage to dare to change your life,

Alexandra

About the Author

Alexandra Vasiliu is an inspirational poet and the bestselling author of *Healing Is a Gift*, *Healing Words*, *Time to Heal*, *Dare to Let Go*, *Blooming*, *Magnetic*, *Be My Moon*, *Through the Heart's Eyes*, and *Plant Hope*.

As an award-winning poet, she uses her imagination to write books that help people overcome life's adversities, heal their emotional wounds, become stronger, and love again. Her poetry touched thousands of people, one heart at a time.

Alexandra double majored in Literature and French for her undergraduate degree before pursuing her Ph.D. in Medieval Literature.

When she isn't busy writing, she can be found in libraries and bookstores browsing books, or outdoors chasing violet sunsets, exploring pine woods, or spending time with her family at the beach.

Get in touch with her on Instagram @alexandravasiliupoetry and Facebook @AlexandraVasiliuWriter. Or, visit her at alexandravasiliu.net.